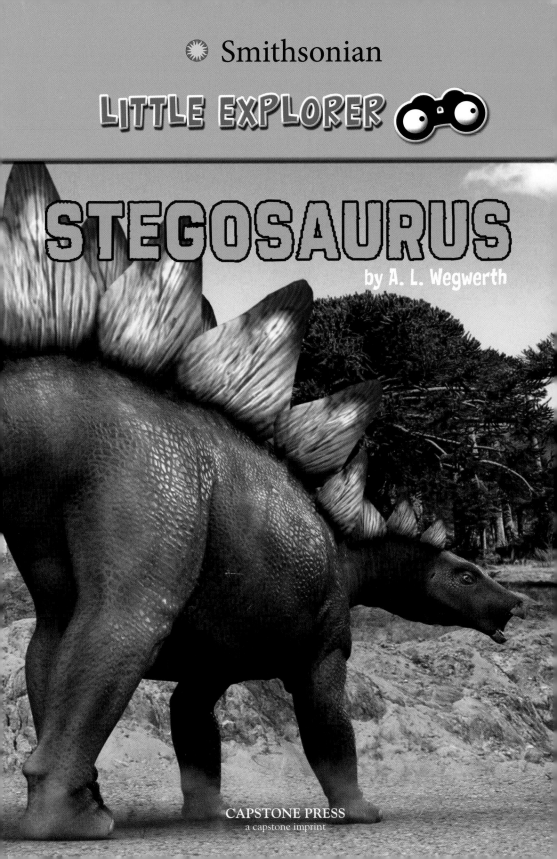

Smithsonian

LITTLE EXPLORER

STEGOSAURUS

by A. L. Wegwerth

CAPSTONE PRESS
a capstone imprint

Little Explorer is published by Capstone Press,
1710 Roe Crest Drive, North Mankato, Minnesota 56003
www.capstonepub.com

**Library of Congress
Cataloging-in-Publication Data**
Wegwerth, A. L., author.
 Stegosaurus / by A.L. Wegwerth.
  pages cm. — (Smithsonian little explorer. Little
paleontologist)
Summary: "Introduces young readers to Stegosaurus,
including physical characteristics, diet, habitat, life cycle,
and the Jurassic period"— Provided by publisher.
 Audience: Ages 4 to 7.
 Audience: K to grade 3.
 Includes index.
 ISBN 978-1-4914-0812-4 (library binding)
 ISBN 978-1-4914-0818-6 (paper over board)
 ISBN 978-1-4914-0824-7 (paperback)
 ISBN 978-1-4914-0830-8 (eBook PDF)
1. Stegosaurus—Juvenile literature. 2. Dinosaurs—
Juvenile literature. I. Title.
 QE862.O65W435 2015
 567.915'3—dc23   2014006191

Editorial Credits
Kristen Mohn, editor; Heidi Thompson, designer;
Wanda Winch, media researcher; Kathy McColley,
production specialist

To Dan —A. L. W.

Our very special thanks to Mike Brett-Surman, PhD,
Museum Specialist for Fossil Dinosaurs, Reptiles,
Amphibians, and Fish at the National Museum of
Natural History, Smithsonian Institution, for his
curatorial review. Capstone would also like to thank
Kealy Wilson, Product Development Manager, and
the following at Smithsonian Enterprises: Ellen
Nanney, Licensing Manager; Brigid Ferraro, Vice
President, Education and Consumer Products;
Carol LeBlanc, Senior Vice President, Education
and Consumer Products.

Image Credits
Capstone: Steve Weston, 14-15; Corel, 4 (bottom left),
16, 17; Dreamstime: Chris Curtis, 28-29, Welcomia,
29 (b); Getty Images Inc: The Bridgeman Art Library,
12-13; Illustrated by Ali Nabavizadeh, 21 (top right);
Jon Hughes, cover, 1, 2-3, 4-5, 8-9, 10,18-19, 20-21,
24-25; Library of Congress: Prints and Photographs
Division, 6 (top); Smithsonian Institution: National
Museum of American History, 7 (b); Peabody Museum
of National History, Yale University, New Haven,
CT, 7 (t); Science Source: Mark Hallett Paleoart, 22-23;
Shutterstock: BACO, 4 (br), Designua, 12 (bottom),
dvektor, 11(bl), reallyround, 5 (tr), Steffen Foerster, 5
(tl), T4W4, 4 (folder), The_Pixel, 6-7 (map), Valentina
Razumova, 18 (bl), Viktorya170377, 11 (t, m, br); www.
dinosauriainternational.com, 26-27, 30-31

Printed in the United States of America in Stevens Point, Wisconsin.
052014   008092WZF14

TABLE OF CONTENTS

name: Stegosaurus

how to say it: steg-uh-SAW-rus

when it lived: late Jurassic Period, Mesozoic Era

what it ate: plants

size: 21 to 30 feet (6.4 to 9 meters) long
12 feet (3.7 m) tall at the hips
weighed 2 to 3 tons
(1.8 to 2.7 metric tons)

Stegosaurus is one of the most recognizable dinosaurs. Its huge size and bony spikes make it hard to miss.

Thanks to FOSSILS

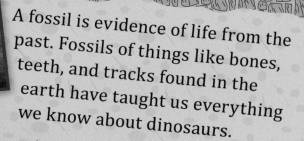

A fossil is evidence of life from the past. Fossils of things like bones, teeth, and tracks found in the earth have taught us everything we know about dinosaurs.

Stegosaurus lived a very long time ago. In fact humans live closer in time to T. rex than T. rex did to Stegosaurus.

THE BONE WARS

The first Stegosaurus fossil was discovered in Colorado in 1876. Othniel Charles Marsh named the dinosaur in 1877. Marsh found Stegosaurus during a time known as the Bone Wars.

Othniel Charles Marsh

Marsh first thought that Stegosaurus might have looked something like a huge turtle.

Colorado

Marsh was racing against another dinosaur hunter, Edward Drinker Cope. Each hoped to find the most dinosaurs. Their race led to many discoveries.

Edward Drinker Cope

The Stegosaurus skeleton Marsh found is at Smithsonian's National Museum of Natural History in Washington, D.C.

SPIKY STEGOSAURUS

bony plates

small skull and brain

narrow,
toothless beak

short front legs

Stegosaurus was one of the first American armored dinosaurs to be discovered.

four-spiked tail

short, broad feet

JURASSIC LIFE

Stegosaurus lived during the late Jurassic Period, 150–145 million years ago. Huge dinosaurs like Brachiosaurus and Diplodocus also roamed the land.

Allosaurus was the main predator of the Jurassic Period. Archaeopteryx—the first flying dinosaur—also lived during this time. It shared the sky with flying reptiles, such as pterodactyls, and many insects.

Archaeopteryx

The Jurassic Period was when mammals first began to increase in size and number.

Other Jurassic Animals

Archaeopteryx

Allosaurus

Diplodocus

Brachiosaurus

The Jurassic Period lasted from 200 million to 145 million years ago.

DINOSAUR ERA

TRIASSIC   JURASSIC   CRETACEOUS

250   200   145   66   present

millions of
years ago

STEGOSAURUS STOMPING GROUND

In the time of dinosaurs, Earth did not look like it does today.

At the beginning of the Triassic Period, there was one supercontinent. It is known as Pangaea. By the Jurassic Period, Pangaea had broken into two continents. One was in the north, and one was in the south.

Earth during the Jurassic Period

Scientists discovered a Stegosaur fossil in Portugal in 2006. It was the first one found outside of North America.

Stegosaurus lived mostly in the northern landmass, which is where part of western North America is today.

The Jurassic Period was very warm and wet. Sea levels were high. Forests full of ferns, cycads, and conifers replaced the deserts of the Triassic Period.

BONY PLATES

Stegosaurus means "roofed lizard."
The name comes from early
paleontologists who thought the
plates looked like shingles on a roof.

Stegosaurus's plates were
covered in keratin. That's the
same material that human
fingernails are made of.

The plates stuck up from the dinosaur's back. They didn't offer any protection to the sides of its body. For this reason scientists believe the plates had purposes besides defense, such as attracting mates.

SOLAR-POWERED DINOSAUR

Scientists now believe Stegosaurus's
plates likely helped the dinosaur
keep a regular body temperature.

Some paleontologists think that the
plates acted like solar panels for heating.

Without plates, Stegosaurus
would have had less area to
take in sun or shade.

Blood pumped through the large plates. This gave more area for the blood to flow near the surface of the dinosaur's skin. The body temperature would quickly cool in the shade or warm up in the sun.

With plates, Stegosaurus had more area to take in sun or shade as needed.

SMALL BRAIN

Stegosaurus is known for its small skull and brain. Because of its small brain, some people think Stegosaurus wasn't very smart. But the species lived for millions of years. Stegosaurus's brain was the perfect size for its kind to survive a very long time.

The brain of Stegosaurus was about half the size of a lime. Compared to its huge body, this was quite tiny!

Meat-eating dinosaurs typically had larger brains than plant-eating dinosaurs like Stegosaurus. Larger brains helped the meat eaters hunt their prey.

PLANT EATER

Stegosaurus was an herbivore. Herbivores eat plants.

At the tip of its snout was a thin, toothless beak, much like a turtle's. The beak was used to chop low-lying bushes and shrubs.

Stegosaurus didn't need a very strong bite for snacking on plants. In fact an alligator has a bite 13 times stronger than a Stegosaurus had!

The sides of Stegosaurus's mouth had many leaf-shaped teeth. They helped crush plants to be swallowed.

STAYING SAFE

Stegosaurus didn't hunt, but that
doesn't mean it didn't face danger.

If faced with a predator, such as Ceratosaurus, Stegosaurus probably didn't run. It stayed put and tried to protect itself.

Stegosaurus was not known to be a fast or nimble dinosaur. Traveling in herds may have helped keep it safe from predators.

ONE TOUGH TAIL

With its spiky plates, you might think
Stegosaurus was well armed against
predators. But most paleontologists
agree that the back plates didn't
provide much protection.

Its powerful spiked tail was probably the
dinosaur's best weapon. It looks stiff,
but scientists think it was quite flexible.

Stegosaurus could swing its tail fast. It may have used its tail to strike predators.

An Allosaurus bone was found with signs of a break from a Stegosaurus spike!

STEGOSAURUS VERSUS ALLOSAURUS

Paleontologists made an amazing discovery in the spring of 2007. Fossils of an Allosaurus and Stegosaurus were found together in Wyoming. The two dinosaurs appeared to be caught in a fight to the death!

Allosaurus skeleton in the Morrison Formation

Allosaurus claw

Allosaurus was a deadly predator. Another discovery included a Stegosaurus fossil with an Allosaurus bite mark in its neck.

FAMOUS FOSSILS

After millions of years, at the end of the Jurassic Period, Stegosaurus became extinct.

Most Stegosaurus fossils have been found in a rocky area of Colorado and Wyoming called the Morrison Formation. It is famous for the number of Jurassic dinosaur fossils discovered there.

"The marvel is not that [the dinosaurs] died out, but that they survived so long."
—paleontologist Richard Swann Lull

a fossil from the Morrison Formation in Colorado

Dinosaur Bone ←

Stegosaurus is Colorado's state fossil because of the many skeleton finds.

GLOSSARY

armor—bones, scales, and skin that some animals have on their bodies for protection

conifer—trees that make cones; conifers are usually evergreen

cycad—a plant shaped like a tall pineapple, with a feathery crown of palmlike leaves

defense—an ability to protect oneself from harm

extinct—no longer living; an extinct species is one that has died out, with no more of its kind

fern—a plant with finely divided leaves known as fronds; ferns are common in damp woods and on mountains

fossil—evidence of life from the geologic past

herbivore—an animal that eats only plants

herd—a large group of animals that lives or moves together

Jurassic—the second period of the Mesozoic Era; when birds first appeared

landmass—a large area of land

Mesozoic Era—the age of dinosaurs, which includes the Triassic, Jurassic, and Cretaceous periods, when the first birds, mammals, and flowers appeared

paleontologist—a scientist who studies fossils

Pangaea—a landmass believed to have once connected all Earth's continents together

plate—a flat, bony growth

predator—an animal that hunts other animals for food

shingle—a flat, thin piece of wood or other material used to cover roofs

skull—the set of bones in the head; the skull protects the brain, eyes, and ears

snout—the long front part of an animal's head; it includes the nose, mouth, and jaws

supercontinent—a large continent that broke into Earth's seven continents

Triassic—the earliest period of the Mesozoic Era; when dinosaurs first appeared

CRITICAL THINKING USING THE COMMON CORE

Study the two dinosaur diagrams on pages 16 and 17. How do the diagrams show how the plates may have helped the dinosaur stay warm? (Craft and Structure)

Read the fact on page 19. Why do you think a hunting animal would need a larger brain than a plant-eating animal? (Key Ideas and Details)

Look at the fact on page 25 about the Allosaurus bone. How does this finding support that Stegosaurus used its tail for defense? (Integration of Knowledge and Ideas)

READ MORE

Bailey, Gerry. *Stegosaurus.* Smithsonian Prehistoric Zone. New York: Crabtree, 2011.

Mara, Wil. *Stegosaurus.* Rookie Read-About Dinosaurs. New York: Children's Press, 2012.

McCurry, Kristen. *How to Draw Incredible Dinosaurs.* Smithsonian. North Mankato, Minn.: Capstone Press, 2013.

INTERNET SITES

FactHound offers a safe, fun way to find Internet sites related to this book. All of the sites on FactHound have been researched by our staff.

Here's all you do:

Visit *www.facthound.com*

Type in this code: 9781491408124

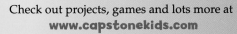

INDEX